HAL•LEONARD
INSTRUMENTAL
PLAY-ALONG

AUDIO
ACCESS
INCLUDED

PLAYBACK+
Speed • Pitch • Balance • Loop

VIOLA

HIP-HOP HITS

Audio arrangements by Peter Deneff

To access audio, visit:
www.halleonard.com/mylibrary

Enter Code
3683-8181-6720-1673

ISBN 978-1-5400-8266-4

HAL•LEONARD®

Visit Hal Leonard Online at
www.halleonard.com

Contact us:
Hal Leonard
7777 West Bluemound Road
Milwaukee, WI 53213
Email: info@halleonard.com

In Europe, contact:
Hal Leonard Europe Limited
42 Wigmore Street
Marylebone, London, W1U 2RN
Email: info@halleonardeurope.com

In Australia, contact:
Hal Leonard Australia Pty. Ltd.
4 Lentara Court
Cheltenham, Victoria, 3192 Australia
Email: info@halleonard.com.au

CONTENTS

BANG BANG
(Rap Version)

VIOLA

Words and Music by ONIKA MARAJ,
MAX MARTIN, SAVAN KOTECHA
and RICKARD GÖRANSSON

With a groove

TALK

VIOLA

Words and Music by KHALID ROBINSON,
GUY LAWRENCE and HOWARD LAWRENCE

R&B Ballad

GOODBYES

VIOLA

Words and Music by AUSTIN POST,
BRIAN LEE, LOUIS BELL,
WILLIAM WALSH, JEFFREY LAMAR WILLIAMS,
VAL BLAVATNIK and JESSIE LAUREN FOUTZ

HOLD UP

VIOLA

Words and Music by BEYONCÉ KNOWLES,
UZOECHI EMENIKE, DEANDRE WAY, DOC POMUS,
MORT SHUMAN, SEAN RHODEN, KAREN ORZOLEK,
NICHOLAS ZINNER, BRIAN CHASE, KELVIN McCONNELL,
ANTONIO RANDOLPH, EMILE HAYNIE, THOMAS PENTZ,
JOSHUA TILLMAN and EZRA KOENIG

JUICE

VIOLA

Words and Music by LIZZO,
THERON MAKIEL THOMAS, ERIC FREDERIC,
SAM SUMSER and SEAN SMALL

LET YOU DOWN

VIOLA

Words and Music by TOMMEE PROFITT
and NATE FEUERSTEIN

LUCID DREAMS

VIOLA

Words and Music by JARAD HIGGINS,
DOMINIC MILLER, GORDON SUMNER,
DANNY SNODGRASS JR. and NICHOLAS MIRA

Moderately slow groove

Guitar

Play

OLD TOWN ROAD

(Remix)

VIOLA

Words and Music by TRENT REZNOR,
BILLY RAY CYRUS, JOCELYN DONALD,
ATTICUS ROSS, KIOWA ROUKEMA
and MONTERO LAMAR HILL

SUCKER FOR PAIN

VIOLA

Words and Music by ALEX GRANT, WAYNE SERMON,
DANIEL REYNOLDS, BENJAMIN McKEE, DANIEL PLATZMAN,
DWAYNE CARTER, ROBERT HALL, CAMERON THOMAZ,
TYRONE WILLIAMS GRIFFIN JR. and SAM HARRIS

SUNFLOWER

from SPIDER-MAN: INTO THE SPIDER-VERSE

VIOLA

Words and Music by AUSTIN RICHARD POST,
CARL AUSTIN ROSEN, KHALIF BROWN,
CARTER LANG, LOUIS BELL
and BILLY WALSH

WORK

VIOLA

Words and Music by ROBYN FENTY,
JAHRON BRATHWAITE, ALLEN RITTER,
AUBREY GRAHAM, MATTHEW SAMUELS,
MONTE S. MOIR and RICHARD STEPHENSON

To Coda ⊕

CODA
⊕

D.S. al Coda

TRUTH HURTS

VIOLA

Words and Music by LIZZO,
ERIC FREDERIC, JESSE ST. JOHN GELLER
and STEVEN CHEUNG